TABLE OF CON

━━━━◆━•◯•━◆━━━━

CHAPTER		PAGE #
	WHY I WROTE THIS BOOK	3
1	YOUR FOCUS IS CORRECTED IN THE PRESENCE OF GOD	5
2	THE PRESENCE OF GOD ENABLES YOU TO SEE THE END RESULT OF YOUR PRESENT DECISION TO SERVE GOD	7
3	THE PRESENCE OF GOD IS CRITICAL TO YOUR SPIRITUAL LIFE	11
4	THE PRESENCE OF GOD WILL BRING REPENTANCE	13
5	THE PRESENCE OF GOD ALWAYS HAS AN EFFECT ON THE UNGODLY	15
6	THE PRESENCE OF GOD CREATES A DIFFERENT REACTION TO DIFFERENT PEOPLE	17
7	IT IS POSSIBLE TO BE IN THE PRESENCE OF GOD AND NOT CHANGE	19
8	HEAVEN AND EARTH RESPOND TO THE PRESENCE OF GOD	21
9	YOU MUST PURSUE THE PRESENCE OF GOD	23

10   THE PRESENCE OF GOD WILL NOT HAPPEN   25
     AUTOMATICALLY IN YOUR LIFE

11   IN THE PRESENCE OF GOD YOU WILL HEAR   29
     CONVERSATIONS THAT YOU WILL NOT HEAR
     ANYWHERE ELSE

12   ENTERING INTO THE PRESENCE OF GOD   33
     REQUIRES OVERCOMING DOUBTS, FEARS
     AND BUSYNESS

13   THE PRESENCE OF GOD CAUSES   37
     ADMIRATION, HUMILITY AND WORSHIP
     IN THE HEART THAT IS TOWARD HIM

14   WE HAVE BEEN GIVEN THE RIGHT TO COME   39
     INTO HIS PRESENCE

15   HUMILITY IS NECESSARY IN ENTERING   41
     HIS PRESENCE

16   MUSIC AND SINGING ARE IMPORTANT FOR   43
     ENTERING HIS PRESENCE

     WISDOM KEYS OF MIKE MURDOCK IN THIS BOOK   45

Unless otherwise indicated, all Scripture quotations are taken from the King James Version of the Bible.

16 Facts About The Presence of God · ISBN 1-56394-322-0/B-233

Copyright © 2010 by **MIKE MURDOCK**

Publisher/Editor: Deborah Murdock Johnson

Published by The Wisdom Center · 4051 Denton Hwy. · Ft. Worth, Texas 76117

1-817-759-BOOK · 1-817-759-2665 · 1-817-759-0300

You Will Love Our Website..! WisdomOnline.com

WHY I WROTE THIS BOOK

<hr/>

What Enters You Determines What Exits You.
Where God is...satan is not.

When Saul became depressed, evil spirits came against his mind, and he brought in the psalmist David.

The Bible says as David began to *play* his harp, the evil spirit left. As David began to *sing* The Holy Spirit entered and the evil spirits were displaced.

"And it came to pass, when the evil spirit from God was upon Saul, that David took an harp, and played with his hand: so Saul was refreshed, and was well, and the evil spirit departed from him," (1 Samuel 16:23).

God Is Not A Presence...He Is A Person With A Presence. His Presence is *evidence* of His Person.

The *quack* is not the *duck.*

The *bark* is not the *dog.*

The Holy Spirit is a Person. He is not *fire...*He *purifies* like fire. He is not *water...*He *cleanses* like water. He is not *wind...*He *moves* like wind.

The Holy Spirit can move suddenly and quickly in your life, *like* wind. "And suddenly there came a sound from Heaven as of a rushing mighty wind, and it filled all the house where they were sitting," (Acts 2:2).

The Bible has much to say about God, the *Person,* the *Aura,* the *Presence* of God.

The Old Testament is different from the New Testament. In the Old Testament The Holy Spirit *visited.* In the New Testament *He stayed.*

In the Old Testament men would suddenly *sense* or *feel* an anointing. Samson *experienced* it.

At one time in Saul's life he became so different

when The Holy Spirit came upon him that people asked, *"Is this the same man?"*

On the Day of Pentecost, after the ascension of Jesus back to Heaven, Jesus said, "And I will pray the Father, and He shall give you another Comforter, that He may abide with you for ever," (John 14:16).

There seems to be two distinct pictures of the Presence of God.

The <u>universal</u> Presence of God refers to the omnipresence of the God we serve.

The Psalmist referred to it, "If I ascend up into Heaven, Thou art there: if I make my bed in hell, behold, Thou art there," (Psalm 139:8).

David said, "Whither shall I go from Thy spirit? or whither shall I flee from Thy presence?" (Psalm 139:7). "Thou hast beset me behind and before, and laid Thine hand upon me," (Psalm 139:5).

The <u>*manifested*</u> Presence of God refers to when you sense Him, feel Him.

There is a Scripture in the Word that talks about God being so real that His very Presence *healed* people.

This seems to indicate there is an *Anointing,* a <u>*Glory*</u> and a <u>*Presence*</u> that is different in meaning.

When you go into a restaurant, it is different than when you go to a Sunday morning service, where people are singing and worshiping God.

It is the manifested Presence when you sense God. You feel a *reaction* in your heart causing you to weep and cry in the Presence of His Glory.

I want you to experience the *Power of His Presence* as you have *never* known it before.

That is why I wrote this book.

Mike Murdock

～ 1 ～

Your Focus Is Corrected In The Presence Of God

The Holy Spirit Imparts Confidence.

When you enter into The Presence of God you see the world differently. The Psalmist put it this way, "I was *angry, bitter* and *discouraged.* I was disheartened when I saw the wicked, the prosperity of ungodly men. Until I went into the sanctuary of God then I understood their end," (see Psalm 73).

"For I was envious at the foolish, when I saw the prosperity of the wicked," (Psalm 73:3).

One Hour In The Presence of God Will Reveal The Flaws of Your Most Carefully Laid Plans.

The Holy Spirit considers you His *dwelling* place. Our tormented thoughts would change if we would remember this verse. "That good thing which was committed unto thee keep by the Holy Ghost which dwelleth in us," (2 Timothy 1:14).

The Holy Spirit provides *tenacity, strength* and *determination* for those who become dependent on His Times of Refreshing Acts and addicted to His Presence.

Doubts are *deadly.* Nothing is more poisonous than the roller coaster emotions regarding your salvation. Satan *taunts, accuses* and *blames* you for everything. "...for the accuser of our brethren is cast down," (Revelation 12:10).

Always remember, The Holy Spirit alone can impart the *unshakable confidence* that Christ dwells within you.

It is The Holy Spirit Who *confirms* that Christ dwells within your heart and removes every doubt about Him. "Hereby know we that we dwell in Him, and He in us, because He hath given us of His Spirit," (1 John 4:13).

The Holy Spirit gives us The Word of God as our special *weapon,* the Sword of the Spirit. "And take the helmet of salvation, and the sword of the Spirit, which is the word of God," (Ephesians 6:17).

The Word of God is the *weapon* that The Holy Spirit uses to *destroy* the works of satan.

Treasure The Word of God. It is the *only* weapon satan cannot withstand.

I encourage you to develop your relationship with The Holy Spirit by daily reading The Word of God. *Talk Scriptures* in every conversation. Timothy instructs us plainly, "Study to shew thyself approved unto God, a workman that needeth not to be ashamed, rightly dividing the word of truth," (2 Timothy 2:15).

Your Focus Is Corrected In The Presence of God.

2

The Presence of God Enables You To See The End Result of Your Present Decision To Serve God

There Are Two Laws of God Operating.

The satanic law where satan offers you the fun things and then... "...the soul that sinneth, it shall die," (Ezekiel 18:4). The way of the transgressor is *hard*. (See Proverbs 13:15.)

Then there is another *Divine* Scriptural law. The law of the bittersweet, where the first part is *bitter* but it ends up *sweet*. "For the end of those things is death," (Romans 6:21).

Jesus said if you are going to follow Me you have to pick up your cross. "Then said Jesus unto His disciples, If any man will come after Me, let him deny himself, and take up his cross, and follow Me," (Matthew 16:24).

In Revelation He tells of the end results...that those who *follow* Him will also *rule* with Him.

Something within you desires a *sense* of *belonging*.

God *knows* where you *belong.*

Something in you finds "belonging" necessary for *comfort, satisfaction* and *rest.*

You are not forgotten by God.

The Holy Spirit is the only One Who can give you the *inner assurance* that you truly are a child of God, *belonging* to the family of God. "The Spirit itself beareth witness with our spirit, that we are the children of God," (Romans 8:16).

When satan reminds you of past failures, remind him of his future failure.

The Holy Spirit sowed the Seeds of Greatness in you. "For ye have not received the spirit of bondage again to fear; but ye have received the Spirit of adoption, whereby we cry, Abba, Father," (Romans 8:15).

Your Heavenly Father has uncommon plans for you. Because you have chosen to serve Him, many *benefits* are awaiting you as you reach for them in faith. "And if children, then heirs; heirs of God, and joint-heirs with Christ; if so be that we suffer with Him, that we may be also glorified together," (Romans 8:17).

Sickness and disease will be defeated because of the faith working within you.

Belonging to God births a hope that will *motivate* you toward purification. "And every man that hath this hope in Him purifieth himself, even as He is pure," (1 John 3:3).

Your faith will grow as you *speak* and *hear* The Word of God continually. "So then faith cometh by hearing, and hearing by the word of God," (Romans 10:17).

Your change of behavior is not the *price* of your relationship with Him, but the *product* of your intimacy with Him.

The Presence of God Enables You To See The End Result of Your Present Decision To Serve God.

RECOMMENDED INVESTMENTS:
The Wisdom Commentary, Vol. 3 (Book/B-228/222 pg)
7 Rewards of The Secret Place (CD/WCPL-84)

The Presence of God Is
The Only Place
Your Weakness Will Die.

-MIKE MURDOCK

❧ 3 ❧

THE PRESENCE OF GOD IS CRITICAL TO YOUR SPIRITUAL LIFE

The Price of God's Presence Is Time.

Paul reminds us in the book of Hebrews the importance of spending time together with other believers. "Not forsaking the assembling of ourselves together, as the manner of some is; but exhorting one another: and so much the more, as ye see the day approaching," (Hebrews 10:25).

Peter said, "...one day is with the Lord as a thousand years, and a thousand years as one day," (2 Peter 3:8).

"My soul longeth, yea, even fainteth for the courts of the Lord: my heart and my flesh crieth out for the living God," (Psalm 84:2).

"But if from thence thou shalt seek the Lord thy God, thou shalt find Him, if thou seek Him with all thy heart and with all thy soul," (Deuteronomy 4:29).

If you have ever wondered, "Why am I here on this planet, earth?" It is time to get close to The Holy Spirit Who will talk to you and *identify* your specific Assignment *designed* specifically for you!

The Holy Spirit will reveal to you the difference between the *essential* and *nonessential* issues. "For it seemed good to the Holy Ghost, and to us, to lay upon you no greater burden than these necessary things," (Acts 15:28).

That is why it is important to have a special place to meet with Him daily. My place is called *The Secret Place.*

You must move away from the voices of others when you really want to hear The Voice of The Holy Spirit. The Holy Spirit will teach you. "He shall teach you all things," (John 14:26).

You can only change when The Holy Spirit is talking into your life.

Solitude is necessary for *intimacy.*
Intimacy is necessary for *impartation.*
Impartation is necessary for *change.*

The Holy Spirit is the very Person Who can answer the questions that perplex you. (See Acts 8.)

The Holy Spirit expects you to continuously listen for His voice. "To day if ye will hear His voice, Harden not your heart," (Psalm 95:7-8).

The Holy Spirit will teach you about things in your Future. "He will shew you things to come," (John 16:13).

You do not know every operation of The Holy Spirit...yet millions are *tasting* the *supernatural* and uncommon events in their communication with Him... *every day of their lives.* You can, too!

The Presence of God Is Critical To Your Spiritual Life.

4

The Presence of God Will Bring Repentance

God's Presence Brings Conviction.

When truth is spoken, *God's Presence* emerges. *It did under Jonah's preaching.* Jonah came to Nineveh and he screamed out "...in forty days, Nineveh [will] be destroyed," (see Jonah 3:4).

The Bible says the people went on a fast and God spared the city. "So the people of Nineveh believed God, and proclaimed a fast, and put on sackcloth, from the greatest of them even to the least of them. And God saw their works, that they turned from their evil way; and God repented of the evil, that He had said that He would do unto them; and He did it not," (Jonah 3:5, 10).

Your Focus Decides Your Feelings.

Jonah's focus was on himself instead of the deliverance of God's people. His choice to change brought about the chance for repentance for many people. The Holy Spirit *woos* and *draws* us toward Him. He is *merciful, gentle* and *kind.* He is *patient, long-suffering* and labors over us as a mother would labor over a child in its tiny crib. His very Presence draws us to a place of repentance.

Respond to His *inner* conviction and drawing power. "Behold, now is the accepted time; behold, now is the day of salvation," (2 Corinthians 6:2).

His Presence keeps you *tender* towards Him. His Presence keeps you *thirsty*. When you do not pursue His Presence, the danger of becoming calloused and hardened is very real. When you feel troubled in your spirit, thank God for such a troubling. Go to Him in *repentance*.

He is waiting to restore you.

Never take His Presence lightly. "I will go and return to My place, till they acknowledge their offence, and seek My face," (Hosea 5:15).

Jesus taught that The Holy Spirit was the secret of *becoming* an Overcomer.

The book of Acts reminds us of the power available to us as believers. "But ye shall receive power, after that the Holy Ghost is come upon you," (Acts 1:8).

You can overcome any temptation, addiction, grief or chaotic situation through The Holy Spirit.

Repent when you have grieved Him.

Let your *dependency* be upon Him and make you the Overcomer you desire to be.

Always remember, The Holy Spirit will reveal specific Wisdom you require for living an overcoming life.

Jesus knew the *anointing* that would enable the disciples to stand against anything. "But ye shall receive power, after that the Holy Ghost is come upon you: and ye shall be witnesses unto Me both in Jerusalem, and in all Judaea, and in Samaria, and unto the uttermost part of the earth," (Acts 1:8).

The Presence of God Will Bring Repentance.

❦ 5 ❦

THE PRESENCE OF GOD ALWAYS HAS AN EFFECT ON THE UNGODLY

Mark People Who Carry A Spirit of Strife.

In the book of Psalms we read, "As smoke is driven away, so drive them away: as wax melteth before the fire, so let the wicked perish at the presence of God," (Psalm 68:2).

In the book of Acts when Stephen began to preach the people became *angry.* He was full of faith, full of The Holy Ghost, but when the people heard his message they *stoned* him to death.

Some who reject correction *repeatedly* must be left alone to the judgments and penalties of God.

The book of Acts says, "Then they cried out with a loud voice, and stopped their ears, and ran upon him with one accord, And cast him out of the city, and stoned him," (Acts 7:57-58).

In Paul's letter to Titus, he wrote, "A man that is an heretic after the first and second admonition reject; Knowing that he that is such is subverted, and sinneth, being condemned of himself," (Titus 3:10-11).

Sometimes those of your own household become your greatest enemies to your own Assignment.

Joseph experienced this when his own brothers sold him as a slave to a passing band of Ishmaelites. The Gospel of Matthew says: "And a man's foes shall be they of his own household," (Matthew 10:36).

Job experienced this through his own wife. In the most devastating tragedy he had ever known, she refused to encourage him. "Then said his wife unto him, Dost thou still retain thine integrity? curse God, and die," (Job 2:9).

Job refused to allow her to influence him away from God. *He fought for his focus.* "But he said unto her, Thou speakest as one of the foolish women speaketh," (Job 2:10).

Sometimes satan uses your closest friends to *scrutinize* your flaws unmercifully to *demoralize* you. The Presence of God can make a difference for you even in the midst of negative situations.

The Presence of God Always Has An Effect On The Ungodly.

RECOMMENDED INVESTMENTS:
The Holy Spirit Handbook (Book/B-100/153 pg)
The Kingly Anointing (CD/WCPL-144)

6

The Presence of God Creates A Different Reaction To Different People

What Some People Love Other People Hate. *What excites some infuriates others.* One day in my office I asked a reporter, who was sneering at a healing crusade that occurred, "Brother don't you believe people are being healed?" He said, "I think *they* think they are being healed."

The Presence of God does not affect everyone the same. The next time you are at church during praise and worship, note the people whose hands are raised. Note the ones who are looking around *sarcastically* and *sneering* at others.

You are a *Door* or a *Wall*. You can become a Wall against *discouragement, cynicism* and *pessimism,* or you can be a Door for others to *walk through* and continue in The Presence of God.

It is sometimes necessary to become a Wall against things that are *unholy, unrighteous* and that bring *unhappiness.*

The Word of God is the instrument of peace for The Holy Spirit to use. As the psalmist David said, "Great peace have they which love Thy law: and nothing shall offend them," (Psalm 119:165).

Fault-finding words create a climate of conflict, anger and cynicism. Warnings can be found in the book of Timothy, "From such turn away," (2 Timothy 3:5).

The Holy Spirit will give you courage and strength to withdraw from the company of foolish people. *When The Holy Spirit becomes your focus, the storm begins to settle in your mind.*

You enter into the rest He promised. "This is the rest wherewith ye may cause the weary to rest; and this is the refreshing," (Isaiah 28:12).

The Proof of Love Is The Willingness To Change. The Holy Spirit is your only Source of true peace. Be willing to pay any price to *protect your focus* and keep your Mind on right things.

The Presence of God Creates A Different Reaction To Different People.

RECOMMENDED INVESTMENTS:
The 3 Most Important Things In Your Life (Book/B-101/240 pg)
The Wisdom Commentary, Vol. 2 (Book/B-220/312 pg)

7

It Is Possible To Be In The Presence of God And Not Change

Men Fail Because of The Words They Speak.

Lucifer was one of the chief angels who was in The Presence of God all the time. He *heard* conversations with God. He *had* conversations with God.

Access Is Always A Test That Produces A Portrait of Character.

As Lucifer stayed in The Presence of God, *Seeds of evil* began to grow in him. He envied God and wanted to take charge and be in a place of power. God did not tolerate that behavior and kicked him and one-third of the angels out of Heaven.

So it is possible to be in the presence of righteousness and not change.

Right words are as important as water on earth and the sustaining of human life. The words of Solomon are, "The words of a man's mouth are as deep waters, and the wellspring of Wisdom as a flowing brook," (Proverbs 18:4).

Because you are a child of the Most High God, you have a right to the *blessings* of God, an *heir* of God, a *joint* heir with Jesus Who is your elder Brother.

But you cannot take hold of the *grace* and *blessings* of God unless you have *knowledge* of what He has provided for you.

The book of Hebrews tells us, "But without faith it is impossible to please Him: for he that cometh to God must believe that He is, and that He is a rewarder of them that diligently seek Him," (Hebrews 11:6).

The Seasons of Your Life Will Change Every Time You Use Your Faith.

Many people have accepted disease and sickness as teachers. The Bible says that The Holy Spirit will lead you into all truth. Not, "Yea I will send disease to teach you and lead you into all truth."

Changes In Your Life Will Always Be Proportionate To Your Knowledge.

You will never stop *negative* thinking until you start *thinking* and *speaking* faith words. You must start believing and seeing yourself *victorious.* That picture will drive out evil.

Champions Make Decisions That Will Create The Future They Desire.

Design The Life You Want. Nobody else can do it for you. Willingness to change is not necessarily a compromise of principles. You must cultivate a teachable spirit, if change is to happen.

It Is Possible To Be In The Presence of God And Not Change.

HEAVEN AND EARTH RESPOND TO THE PRESENCE OF GOD

The Very Heavens Move At His Command.
In the book of Psalms...we read about the mighty power of God. "The earth shook, the Heavens also dropped at the presence of God: even Sinai itself was moved at the presence of God, the God of Israel," (Psalm 68:8).

The disciples were with Jesus in the boat when a storm arose. The disciples were concerned so they called out to Jesus Who was *sleeping...*

Jesus spoke and the winds obeyed Him. "And He saith unto them, Why are ye fearful, O ye of little faith? Then He arose, and rebuked the winds and the sea; and there was a great calm," (Matthew 8:26).

He speaks to the earth and the Heavens. "Give ear, O ye Heavens, and I will speak; and hear, O earth, the words of My mouth," (Deuteronomy 32:1).

The Heavens and earth are commanded to rejoice. "Let the Heavens be glad, and let the earth rejoice: and let men say among the nations, The Lord reigneth," (1 Chronicles 16:31).

God is worshiped by the host of Heaven. "Thou,

even Thou, art Lord alone; Thou hast made Heaven, the Heaven of Heavens, with all their host, the earth, and all things that are therein, the seas, and all that is therein, and Thou preservest them all; and the host of Heaven worshippeth Thee," (Nehemiah 9:6).

The winds obey God as He protects His children, the Israelites. "And the Lord turned a mighty strong west wind, which took away the locusts, and cast them into the Red sea; there remained not one locust in all the coasts of Egypt," (Exodus 10:19).

God gives the rainbow as a token of promise. "I do set My bow in the cloud, and it shall be for a token of a covenant between Me and the earth," (Genesis 9:13).

How do we know God exists? "The Heavens declare the glory of God; and the firmament sheweth His handywork," (Psalm 19:1).

Heaven And Earth Respond To The Presence of God.

RECOMMENDED INVESTMENTS:
The God Book (Book/B-26/160 pg)
The Holy Spirit Handbook (Book/B-100/153 pg)

9

You Must Pursue The Presence of God

God Does Require Pursuit.
The Holy Spirit is the only Friend Who can *change* your very nature.

He will give you focus and turn you from a child of *disobedience* into a child of *light.*

The Bible says, draw near to God and He will draw near to you. "But it is good for me to draw near to God: I have put my trust in the Lord God, that I may declare all Thy works," (Psalm 73:28). Jesus said, "Come unto Me, all ye that labour and are heavy laden, and I will give you rest," (Matthew 11:28).

When your pursuit of His Kingdom becomes your *priority,* everything else you need in life will emerge. "But seek ye first the kingdom of God, and His righteousness; and all these things shall be added unto you," (Matthew 6:33).

You cannot enter life in the Spirit without *respecting* The Holy Spirit. *He goes where He is desired, not merely where He is needed.*

Millions are staggering around the earth like drunkards *emotionally* bankrupt, *spiritually* sabotaged, helpless and *lost.*

Only The Holy Spirit can move them from

darkness into light. You may feel *alone,* isolated and even have *tormenting* thoughts that nobody really cares for you at all.

But the opposite is occurring.

The Holy Spirit is continuously talking to the Father about your *needs* and *desires.*

The Holy Spirit is in total agreement with the desires and will of the Father for *you.* Your Heavenly Father hears the cry of your heart. "And He that searcheth the hearts knoweth what is the mind of the Spirit, because He maketh intercession for the saints according to the will of God," (Romans 8:27).

Let your words become *photographs* of the Future you *desire,* instead of the Future you *fear.*

1. *Talk* like an overcomer.
2. *Think* like an overcomer.
3. *Laugh* like a victor, not a victim.

His biggest plans will come to pass in your life.

You Must Pursue The Presence of God.

RECOMMENDED INVESTMENTS:
The God Book (Book/B-26/160 pg)
The Wisdom Commentary, Vol. 3 (Book/B-228/222 pg)
7 Rewards of The Secret Place (CD/WCPL-84)

≈ **10** ≈

THE PRESENCE OF GOD WILL NOT HAPPEN AUTOMATICALLY IN YOUR LIFE

The Price of God's Presence Is Time.

Jesus would have walked right by the blind man had he not cried out, "Jesus, Thou son of David, have mercy on me," (Mark 10:47). "And, behold, two blind men sitting by the way side, when they heard that Jesus passed by, cried out, saying, Have mercy on us, O Lord, Thou Son of David," (Matthew 20:30).

The Magnet For His Presence Will Be Your Faith And Pursuit.

The woman who had hemorrhaged for 12 years would have never gotten into His Presence had she not pressed through the crowd. "And, behold, a woman, which was diseased with an issue of blood twelve years, came behind Him, and touched the hem of His garment," (Matthew 9:20).

You Can Change Your Life. Believe it or not, you can. Regardless of your family situation, your financial status or past failures, you can step up into a "Victory Zone" and stay excited about life. God "...hath raised us up together, and made us sit together in Heavenly places in Christ Jesus," (Ephesians 2:6).

Correct and enlarge your picture of God by reading good books, listening to teaching CDs and sharing your love with others.

Spend time developing the proper concept of God. Rebuild the '*Mind Photo*' that strengthens your faith toward Him.

Your destiny requires your own decision-making. Failures occur daily. You will fail too, unless you learn the art of *motivating yourself.* Destiny necessitates your involvement.

This is a Scriptural principle.

Read this promise, "If ye be willing and obedient, ye shall eat the good of the land: But if ye refuse and rebel, ye shall be devoured with the sword," (Isaiah 1:19-20).

The greatest book on the earth is The Bible. It has outsold every other book in the world. It is The Word of God. *The Word of God will keep you pure.* "Wherewithal shall a young man cleanse his way? by taking heed thereto according to Thy word," (Psalm 119:9).

Belonging to God will require your faith in Jesus Christ. "For ye are all the children of God by faith in Christ Jesus," (Galatians 3:26). Always remember The Holy Spirit will reveal specific Wisdom you require for living an overcoming life.

The Holy Spirit will teach you step-by-step how to enter into the supernatural prayer life.

Value and celebrate moments in His Presence. Be willing to be changed and make new discoveries. *Pursue* Him. *He is the Spirit of Truth.*

Jesus wants to rule every part of your life and

guide you in making the right decisions. He does this through The Holy Spirit Who is our *Advisor, Comforter* and *Friend* Who never leaves us nor forsakes us.

Your personal *circumstances* are created by your *Decisions* and your own *Passion.*

The Presence of God Will Not Happen Automatically In Your Life.

RECOMMENDED INVESTMENTS:
Where Miracles Are Born (Book/B-115/32 pg)
The Wisdom Commentary, Vol. 1 (Book/B-136/256 pg)
5 Keys To Birthing Your Daily Habit of Prayer (CD/WCPL-85)

The Holy Spirit Is The Only One You Are Required To Obey.

-MIKE MURDOCK

≈ 11 ≈

In The Presence of God You Will Hear Conversations That You Will Not Hear Anywhere Else

God Is A Communicator.
God talks. He created the mouth…the tongue.

God is such a communicator that everything He created has ears. He said that you can talk to the mountain and it will move if you have faith. "Jesus answered and said unto them, Verily I say unto you, If ye have faith, and doubt not, ye shall not only do this which is done to the fig tree, but also if ye shall say unto this mountain, Be thou removed, and be thou cast into the sea; it shall be done," (Matthew 21:21).

Angels talk with Him.

"And the angel answering said unto Him, I am Gabriel, that stand in the presence of God; and am sent to speak unto Thee, and to shew Thee these glad tidings," (Luke 1:19). Romans chapter 8 talks about The Holy Spirit discussing us with the Father and interpreting our prayer language with groanings that cannot be uttered.

Right now in the Heavens, Jesus makes intercession for us. He is talking to the Father for us. "Likewise the Spirit also helpeth our infirmities: for we know not what we should pray for as we ought: but the Spirit itself maketh intercession for us with groanings which cannot be uttered," (Romans 8:26).

He is a visual God. He showed Abraham *pictures* of his future greatness. "And I will make of thee a great nation, and I will bless thee, and make thy name great; and thou shalt be a blessing: And I will bless them that bless thee, and curse him that curseth thee: and in thee shall all families of the earth be blessed," (Genesis 12:2-3).

He thinks. "For I know the thoughts that I think toward you, saith the Lord, thoughts of peace, and not of evil, to give you an expected end," (Jeremiah 29:11).

Every act of God is designed to *increase* your *dependency* upon Him and your *addiction* to His Presence. "And He humbled thee, and suffered thee to hunger, and fed thee with manna, which thou knewest not, neither did thy fathers know; that He might make thee know that man doth not live by bread only, but by every word that proceedeth out of the mouth of the Lord doth man live," (Deuteronomy 8:3).

Does He express anger? "God judgeth the righteous, and God is angry with the wicked every day," (Psalm 7:11).

What would He say about His will for you? "Trust in the Lord with all thine heart; and lean not unto thine own understanding," (Proverbs 3:5).

He expresses His opinion about sickness and disease. "For I will restore health unto thee, and I will heal thee of thy wounds, saith the Lord," (Jeremiah 30:17).

Does He know your Future? "Before I formed thee in the belly I knew thee; and before thou camest forth out of the womb I sanctified thee, and I ordained thee a prophet unto the nations," (Jeremiah 1:5).

He not only speaks, thinks, predicts and loves us... He gives us a promise. He has said, "...I will never leave thee, nor forsake thee," (Hebrews 13:5).

When He talks, each word is an invitation to a Miracle. "Give, and it shall be given unto you; good measure, pressed down, and shaken together, and running over, shall men give into your bosom. For with the same measure that ye mete withal it shall be measured to you again," (Luke 6:38).

He will be your Mentor day-by-day in your Assignment. God will *qualify* you. "And the Lord said unto him...Now therefore go, and I will be with thy mouth, and teach thee what thou shalt say," (Exodus 4:11-12).

In The Presence of God You Will Hear Conversations That You Will Not Hear Anywhere Else.

RECOMMENDED INVESTMENTS:
The God Book (Book/B-26/160 pg)
The Assignment (The Dream & The Destiny), Vol. 1
 (Book/B-74/164 pg)

What You Do Daily
Determines What You
Become Permanently.

-MIKE MURDOCK

~ 12 ~

ENTERING INTO THE PRESENCE OF GOD REQUIRES OVERCOMING DOUBTS, FEARS AND BUSYNESS

The Holy Spirit In Your Life Will Dispel Fear.

Your chosen *focus* is the world you have *created* for yourself.

God speaks to Moses. "Behold, the Lord thy God hath set the land before thee: go up and possess it, as the Lord God of thy fathers hath said unto thee; fear not, neither be discouraged," (Deuteronomy 1:21).

People drain you.

Battles drain you. You must go back to The Holy Spirit for rejuvenation.

Jesus promised that the *power* would come to us through The Holy Spirit. "He giveth power to the faint; and to them that have no might He increaseth strength," (Isaiah 40:29). "Come unto Me, all ye that labour and are heavy laden, and I will give you rest," (Matthew 11:28).

It is The Holy Spirit Who confirms that Christ dwells within your heart and removes every doubt about

Him. "Hereby know we that we dwell in Him, and He in us, because He hath given us of His Spirit," (1 John 4:13).

Love is an enemy of fear.

Fear *torments* and increases the size of your enemy *mentally*. When love fills your heart, fear has no place in your life. "There is no fear in love; but perfect love casteth out fear: because fear hath torment. He that feareth is not made perfect in love," (1 John 4:18).

The fruit of The Holy Spirit is love. "But the fruit of the Spirit is love, joy, peace, longsuffering, gentleness, goodness, faith," (Galatians 5:22).

Your life in the Spirit will cause fear to *dissolve* and be *dispelled* from your life.

God is the One Who delivers. "But the Lord your God ye shall fear; and He shall deliver you out of the hand of all your enemies," (2 Kings 17:39).

Come into His Presence. Reach out toward The Holy Spirit. Ask Him to *remove* every ounce of fear within you. Begin to thank Jesus for paying the price, making you an Overcomer, and interceding for you before the Father. "And it shall come to pass in the day that the Lord shall give thee rest from thy sorrow, and from thy fear, and from the hard bondage wherein thou wast made to serve," (Isaiah 14:3).

God gives deliverance from fear and bondage.

Skilled negotiators teach that *waiting* is a *weapon*. Whoever is the most hurried and impatient usually ends up with the worst end of the deal.

Take time to do things right.

Jesus never hurried. This was one of the Leadership Secrets of Jesus. A Psalm of David says, "The king shall joy in Thy strength, O Lord; and in Thy salvation how greatly shall he rejoice!" (Psalm 21:1).

What You Do Daily Determines What You Become Permanently.

Entering Into The Presence of God Requires Overcoming Doubts, Fears And Busyness.

RECOMMENDED INVESTMENTS:
The Double Diamond Principle (Book/B-39/148 pg)
The Making of A Champion (Book/B-59/128 pg)
The Leadership Secrets of Jesus (Book/B-91/196 pg)

The Proof of Humility
Is The Willingness
To Reach.

-*MIKE MURDOCK*

❧ 13 ❧

THE PRESENCE OF GOD CAUSES ADMIRATION, HUMILITY AND WORSHIP IN THE HEART THAT IS TOWARD HIM

Worship Is The Correction of Focus.
Angels worship and magnify Him.

According to the book of Revelation, angels fall prostrate in Heaven when they come into His Presence. "The four and twenty elders fall down before Him that sat on the throne, and worship Him that liveth for ever and ever, and cast their crowns before the throne, saying, Thou art worthy, O Lord, to receive glory and honour and power: for Thou hast created all things, and for Thy pleasure they are and were created," (Revelation 4:10-11).

The Proof of Humility Is The Willingness To Reach. "And, behold, a woman, which was diseased with an issue of blood twelve years, came behind Him, and touched the hem of His garment: For she said within herself, If I may but touch His garment, I shall be whole," (Matthew 9:20-21).

There was an inner trust and worshipful desire for

the Son of God as she reached for Him.

The queen of Sheba recognized the Wisdom and Presence of God in her visit with Solomon. She demonstrated great *reverence* and *admiration* for him. Read about this encounter in 1 Kings 10.

The Holy Spirit knows specifically what you need during times of mental anguish and confusion. David cried out after his own terrible sin with Bathsheba. "Cast me not away from Thy presence; and take not Thy holy spirit from me," (Psalm 51:11).

It was a remarkable *work of grace* in the human heart when The Holy Spirit enabled Stephen to *love* those who stoned him. "And he kneeled down, and cried with a loud voice, Lord, lay not this sin to their charge," (Acts 7:60).

Many wives have birthed the salvation of their husbands because of the love of The Holy Spirit within them. Thousands of rebellious teenagers have been drawn back home like a *magnet* to a loving parent... because of the *love* of The Holy Spirit.

The Holy Spirit alone could plant this kind of love inside a human heart.

The Holy Spirit tests your appetite and pursuit of Him. "God looked down from Heaven upon the children of men, to see if there were any that did understand, that did seek God," (Psalm 53:2). "For the eyes of the Lord run to and fro throughout the whole earth, to shew Himself strong in the behalf of them whose heart is perfect toward Him," (2 Chronicles 16:9). *The Holy Spirit looks upon you to find a reason to bless you.*

The Presence of God Causes Admiration, Humility And Worship In The Heart That Is Toward Him.

❦ 14 ❦

We Have Been Given The Right To Come Into His Presence

God Requires Obedience.

In the Old Testament when the high priest was going into the Holy of Holies to offer up sacrifices for the people, he would have a rope around his ankle.

If God would not accept the sacrifice then He would have to kill the high priest. The people would then have to pull him out by the rope because *nobody* was *allowed* to enter into the Holy of Holies.

When Jesus was crucified, The Bible says that the veil of the temple was rent from the top to the bottom. *It is significant the writer tells us how the veil was rent.* That meant *anyone* could approach God. *Anyone had access to God.*

It was not torn from the bottom to the top with man forcing his way to God.

The veil of the temple was ripped from the top to the bottom. It meant that God had literally created a way so that man could come to Him. "And, behold, the veil of the temple was rent in twain from the top to the bottom; and the earth did quake, and the rocks rent," (Matthew 27:51).

The Holy Spirit imparts inner confidence that you belong to the family of God.

God wants to be your Father even more than you want to be His child. "The Spirit itself beareth witness with our spirit, that we are the children of God," (Romans 8:16).

The Holy Spirit wants to anoint you for the work He has called you to do. "Ask, and it shall be given you; seek, and ye shall find; knock, and it shall be opened unto you: For every one that asketh receiveth; and he that seeketh findeth; and to him that knocketh it shall be opened," (Matthew 7:7-8).

Your *success* is not limited to your efforts.

Your *Future* is not limited by your personal knowledge.

Your *victories* are not dependent on your own personal abilities alone.

The Holy Spirit and Jesus are your *Personal Intercessors* throughout every trial and difficult place of your life.

The Holy Spirit is ever working in your behalf, because of the love of the Father for your life. "No good thing will He withhold from them that walk uprightly," (Psalm 84:11).

The Holy Spirit *knows* where you belong. He knows the person that He created you to be. "He found him in a desert land, and in the waste howling wilderness; He led him about, He instructed him, He kept him as the apple of His eye," (Deuteronomy 32:10).

You truly are the apple of your Father's eye.

We Have Been Given The Right To Come Into His Presence.

≈ 15 ≈

Humility Is Necessary In Entering His Presence

———⬧◦⬧———

What You Respect, You Will Attract.

Never become cocky. In the book of Job he says, "If I could find God, I would argue with Him."

My mother always told me as long as you have that *attitude* God will not be *accessible.* "Oh that I knew where I might find Him! that I might come even to His seat! I would order my cause before Him, and fill my mouth with arguments," (Job 23:3-4).

Acknowledge that you do not know everything. Admit you do not always know how to pray effectively through your own logic and Mind. "Lord, Thou hast heard the desire of the humble: Thou wilt prepare their heart, Thou wilt cause Thine ear to hear," (Psalm 10:17).

It is important to avoid any criticism of those who carry the anointing of The Holy Spirit. "Touch not Mine anointed, and do My prophets no harm," (Psalm 105:15).

It is a dangerous thing to treat lightly that supernatural Anointing. "A man's pride shall bring him low: but honour shall uphold the humble in spirit," (Proverbs 29:23).

The Holy Spirit chooses the person He anoints.

Men do not choose that anointing. Treasure the moment The Holy Spirit anoints and does something specific and unique through you.

Humbly thank Him for the privilege of being used to bring healing to the broken. "Whosoever therefore shall humble himself as this little child, the same is greatest in the kingdom of Heaven," (Matthew 18:4).

The greatest warfare of your life is The Holy Spirit versus your flesh and self. "For the flesh lusteth against the Spirit, and the Spirit against the flesh: and these are contrary the one to the other: so that ye cannot do the things that ye would," (Galatians 5:17).

You will stand before God and give an account for every response you have made to the inner voice of The Holy Spirit. "So then every one of us shall give account of himself to God," (Romans 14:12).

It is a dangerous moment to think that access to God is permanent and easy. "If My people, which are called by My name, shall humble themselves, and pray, and seek My face, and turn from their wicked ways; then will I hear from Heaven, and will forgive their sin, and will heal their land," (2 Chronicles 7:14).

Jesus showed humility. "But made Himself of no reputation, and took upon Him the form of a servant, and was made in the likeness of men," (Philippians 2:7).

Never Take His Presence Lightly.
Humility Is Necessary In Entering His Presence.

❧ 16 ❧

Music And Singing Are Important For Entering His Presence

***

Come Before His Presence Singing.

Come into His Presence *Rejoicing* and with *Thanksgiving.* (See Psalm 100:1-4.)

God will never dwell in a joyless environment. If you want His Presence in your life, you must sing to Him. "Serve the Lord with gladness: come before His presence with singing," (Psalm 100:2).

Worship Corrects Focus.

Music is the entry into the spirit world, evil or Holy. A song is protocol for entering into His Presence.

If you sing to The Holy Spirit, He will enter. When you are going through an attack, sing. When you sing, worship and magnify God, satan has memories of being the *ex*-choir director of Heaven and is *demoralized.* When you *sing,* he cannot stay in your presence.

When you *magnify* God, *He will manifest His Presence.* Today in many ministries where there is a great move of The Holy Spirit there is always singing and worshiping. *Your singing is an act of obedience to The Holy Spirit.*

Create a Secret Place at your home. It is a place to

meet with The Holy Spirit. Where you are matters as much as what you are. *Where You Are Determines What Dies Within You.*

Meet with Him at the same time every morning. Pursue His Presence. Do it for 30 days. Come into His Presence singing to Him, loving on Him.

Write down your impressions. Take *The Seeds of Wisdom Topical Bible* with you, and read the Scripture for that day. Nurture your relationship with Him because in His Presence is fullness of joy. "...in Thy presence is fulness of joy; at Thy right hand there are pleasures for evermore," (Psalm 16:11).

Music And Singing Are Important For Entering His Presence.

Our Prayer Together...

"Father, You said You would deliver us *according to our faith,* so today, shut the mouths of the lions. Silence every gainsayer, every false accusation. In Jesus' name, *help us to rise above the circumstances.*

We trust You. We trust Your Word. In Jesus' name. Amen."

Wisdom Keys of Mike Murdock In This Book

1. Access Is Always A Test That Produces A Portrait of Character.
2. Champions Make Decisions That Will Create The Future They Desire.
3. Changes In Your Life Will Always Be Proportionate To Your Knowledge.
4. God Is Not A Presence...He Is A Person With A Presence.
5. It Is Possible To Be In The Presence of God And Not Change.
6. One Hour In The Presence of God, Will Reveal The Flaws of Your Most Carefully Laid Plans.
7. The Holy Spirit Is The Only One You Are Required To Obey.
8. The Magnet For His Presence Will Be Your Faith And Pursuit.
9. The Presence of God Does Not Affect Everyone The Same.
10. The Presence of God Is The Only Place Your Weakness Will Die.
11. The Presence of God Will Not Happen Automatically In Your Life.
12. The Price of God's Presence Is Time.
13. The Proof of Humility Is The Willingness To Reach.
14. The Proof of Love Is The Willingness To Change.
15. The Seasons of Your Life Will Change Every Time You Use Your Faith.
16. What Enters You Determines What Exits You.
17. What You Do Daily Determines What You Become Permanently.
18. Where You Are Determines What Dies Within You.
19. Your Focus Decides Your Feelings.

DECISION

Will You Accept Jesus As Your Personal Savior Today?

The Bible says, "That if thou shalt confess with thy mouth the Lord Jesus, and shalt believe in thine heart that God hath raised Him from the dead, thou shalt be saved," (Romans 10:9).

Pray this prayer from your heart today!

"Dear Jesus, I believe that You died for me and rose again on the third day. I confess I am a sinner...I need Your love and forgiveness...Come into my heart. Forgive my sins. I receive Your eternal life. Confirm Your love by giving me peace, joy and supernatural love for others. Amen."

DR. MIKE MURDOCK

is in tremendous demand as one of the most dynamic speakers in America today.

More than 17,000 audiences in over 100 countries have attended his Schools of Wisdom and conferences. Hundreds of invitations come to him from churches, colleges and business corporations. He is a noted author of over 250 books, including the best sellers, *The Leadership Secrets of Jesus* and *Secrets of the Richest Man Who Ever Lived.* Thousands view his weekly television program, *Wisdom Keys with Mike Murdock.* Many attend his Schools of Wisdom that he hosts in many cities of America.

Clip and Mail

☐ Yes, Mike! I made a decision to accept Christ as my personal Savior today. Please send me my free gift of your book, *31 Keys to a New Beginning* to help me with my new life in Christ.

NAME _____ BIRTHDAY _____

ADDRESS _____

CITY _____ STATE ____ ZIP _____

PHONE _____ E-MAIL _____

Mail to: **The Wisdom Center** · 4051 Denton Hwy. · Ft. Worth, TX 76117
1-817-759-BOOK · 1-817-759-2665 · 1-817-759-0300
You Will Love Our Website..! WisdomOnline.com

46

DR. MIKE MURDOCK

Has embraced his Assignment to Pursue...Proclaim...and Publish the Wisdom of God to help people achieve their dreams and goals.

Preached his first public sermon at the age of 8.

Preached his first evangelistic crusade at the age of 15.

Began full-time evangelism at the age of 19, which has continued since 1966.

Has traveled and spoken to more than 17,000 audiences in over 100 countries, including East and West Africa, Asia, Europe and South America.

Noted author of over 250 books, including best sellers, *Wisdom for Winning, Dream Seeds, The Double Diamond Principle, The Law of Recognition* and *The Holy Spirit Handbook.*

Created the popular *Topical Bible* series for Businessmen, Mothers, Fathers, Teenagers; *The One-Minute Pocket Bible* series, and *The Uncommon Life* series.

The Creator of The Master 7 Mentorship System, an Achievement Program for Believers.

Has composed thousands of songs such as "I Am Blessed," "You Can Make It," "God Rides On Wings Of Love" and "Jesus, Just The Mention Of Your Name," recorded by many gospel artists.

Is the Founder and Senior Pastor of The Wisdom Center, in Fort Worth, Texas...a Church with International Ministry around the world.

Host of *Wisdom Keys with Mike Murdock,* a weekly TV Program seen internationally.

Has appeared often on TBN, CBN, BET, Daystar, Inspirational Network, LeSea Broadcasting and other television network programs.

Has led over 3,000 to accept the call into full-time ministry.

THE MINISTRY

1 **Wisdom Books & Literature** - Over 250 best-selling Wisdom Books and 70 Teaching CD Series.

2 **Church Crusades** - Multitudes are ministered to in crusades and seminars throughout America in "The Uncommon Wisdom Conferences." Known as a man who loves pastors he has focused on church crusades for over 43 years.

3 **Music Ministry** - Millions have been blessed by the anointed songwriting and singing of Mike Murdock, who has made over 15 music albums and CDs available.

4 **Television** - *Wisdom Keys with Mike Murdock,* a nationally-syndicated weekly television program.

5 **The Wisdom Center** - The Church and Ministry Offices where Dr. Murdock speaks weekly on Wisdom for The Uncommon Life.

6 **Schools of The Holy Spirit** - Mike Murdock hosts Schools of The Holy Spirit in many churches to mentor believers on the Person and Companionship of The Holy Spirit.

7 **Schools of Wisdom** - In many major cities Mike Murdock hosts Schools of Wisdom for those who want personalized and advanced training for achieving "The Uncommon Dream."

8 **Missions Outreach** - Dr. Mike Murdock's overseas outreaches to over 100 countries have included crusades in East and West Africa, Asia, Europe and South America.